WATERLOO LOCAL S... Y0-CJJ-169
MIDDLE SCHOOL LIBRARY

781 DWE

*Let's Look At
Series
Edited by Robert Owen*

LET'S LOOK AT
Musical Instruments *and the* Orchestra

LET'S LOOK AT
Musical Instruments
and the Orchestra

C. O. Rhodes, M.A.

Foreword by
Sir Malcolm Sargent

Illustrated by
Norma Ost

ALBERT WHITMAN & Company
Chicago

Standard Book Number 8075-4483-3
Library of Congress Card Number 71-85229
First published in Great Britain in 1968 by
Frederick Muller Limited
Copyright © 1968 by C. O. Rhodes
First published in the United States by
Albert Whitman & Company

Also in this series:
Let's Look At CASTLES *Alan R. Warwick*
COSTUMES *Edmund J. Cooper*
HOUSES AND HOMES *Joan Morey*
PREHISTORIC ANIMALS
Alan R. Warwick
PUPPETS *A. R. Philpott*
SHIPS *Gerald Bowman*
TRAINS *Ernest F. Carter*

Editor: Robert Owen

FOREWORD

Mr. Rhodes' fascinating little book should be of interest to all lovers of music both young and old.

It is an error of the unobservant to believe that only the howls and bangs of 'pop' music appeal to the young. Promenade audiences and the record clubs all over the world prove the contrary to be true.

In this book we have a succinct history of the development of the instruments for music-making, and a clear description of the many instruments of the modern orchestra. I am sure that the reader will find an added interest and enjoyment in his concert-going or 'home-listening', but my hope is that he will be excited to undertake the playing of an instrument, first of all for his own pleasure, and secondly for the pleasure he can give other people. We need more professional orchestras (which means the employment of more musicians), and I cannot exaggerate the joy of amateur communal music-making.

Malcolm Sargent

HOW MUSIC BEGAN

All the world over people love making music. There has scarcely ever been known a tribe or a community so poor or so backward that it has not possessed musical instruments of some kind, however primitive.

It has always been so. In prehistoric times, twenty-five thousand years ago, men bored through the foot bones of the reindeer to produce pipes with which they could make musical sounds. Relics of such pipes have been found in the remains of ancient dwellings.

Later, men stretched skins over bowls made of clay to fashion their drums. In the Bronze Age they hammered sheets of metal into the shape of elephants' tusks and blew through them to make a rousing blast.

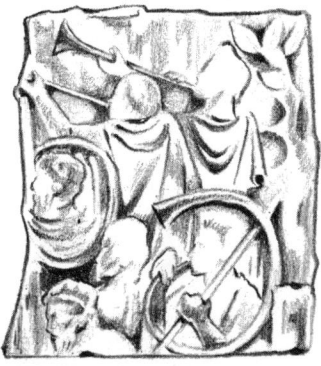

Roman Trumpets: from Trajan's Column Rome, first century A.D.

In those times people did not, as we do, listen to their instruments for the sake of their musical quality alone. They had a more practical intention. Some of the sounds they made were probably far from pleasant. But they were believed to have magic power to drive away the evil spirits and attract the good. Music was much used in religious ceremonies. That is still true. Throughout the ages some of the finest music has always been that which was composed for temples and churches.

A Greek lyre

Some of the early instruments would not produce more than two or three notes. As centuries passed musicians learned how to increase their range or compass and vary their quality. They took pride in their instruments as masterpieces of artistry and craftsmanship.

In classical times the Greeks had, for instance, the *kithara*, an instrument of eleven strings that was played by plucking the strings with the fingers of both hands. Not only was this used for the accompaniment of singing and reciting, it was used also as a solo instrument. Competitions for performers were held at the Delphic Games. A Greek wind instrument, the *aulos*, had a range of two and a half octaves and was used as an accompaniment to plays at the theatre.

Greek aulos player and dancing girl

Assyrian lyre

In the Roman Empire, as would be expected, military music was much in demand. Two trumpet-like instruments, the *tuba* and the *cornu*, were used in the army for signalling.

When the Roman Empire collapsed the music of ancient times died with it. It was over a thousand years later before the instruments we hear in a modern orchestra began to take their present form. Even during the last three hundred years big improvements have been made in them.

Roman buccina

Man with recorder, fifteenth century

HOW MUSICAL SOUNDS ARE MADE

Before we can understand the instruments of the modern orchestra we need to know how musical sounds are produced. A simple experiment will help to explain this.

Take a rubber band and stretch it as far as possible without breaking it. Now pluck the rubber band sharply in the middle. The rubber band will visibly vibrate, giving out a twang as it does so. While the vibration is dying away toward the middle of the rubber band, the twanging sound will rise in pitch.

This occurs because the vibration of the rubber band starts series of corresponding vibrations in the air that spread out like the wavelets when a stone is thrown into a pond. These, in turn, cause the eardrum of the listener to vibrate.

But notice this: if a cork is floating on the surface of a pond when a stone is thrown it is not carried away. It just bobs up and down. It is the same with the molecules of the air. They do not travel but just bob about in the same place, passing on their disturbance to the surrounding molecules. These, in their turn, pass on the vibrations to the molecules nearest to them. So the process continues in ever widening circles.

Vibrations such as this are known as 'transverse vibrations'. The longer the rubber band, the slower are the vibrations and the lower is the note produced. It is the rise in pitch of the note as the vibrations die away toward the center of the band that gives the sound its charm. It is in this way that the sound is different from the mere noise made when a small boy amuses himself, but nobody else, by banging two pot lids together.

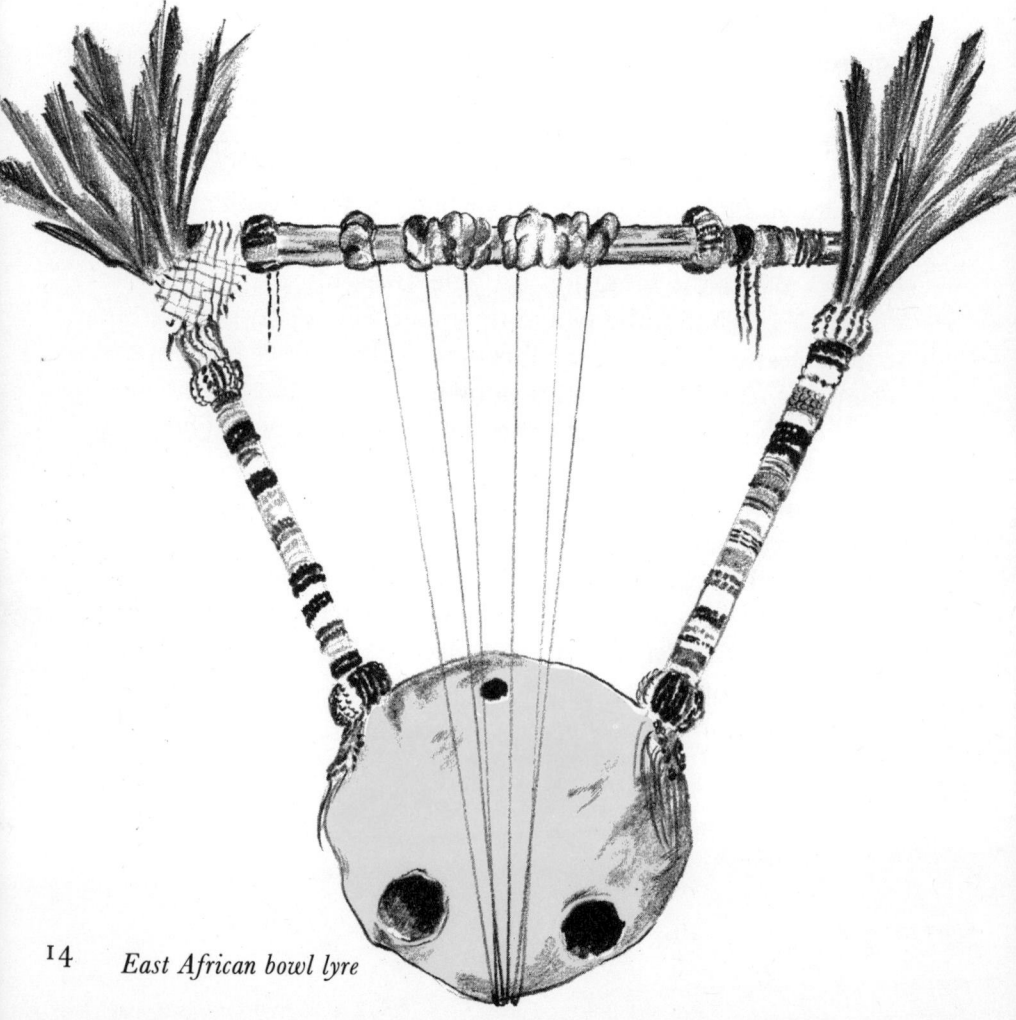

East African bowl lyre

Stringed instruments and drums cause vibrations of this kind. But there is another type of vibration that also results in beautiful sound.

Imagine a long train standing in a railroad yard. If the engine gives a sudden jerk, it sends the cars clashing one against the next all the way to the caboose. Then the cars all come clanging back on their couplings. Blowing hard down a tube causes the molecules in the air to push each other to and fro in much the same way. These vibrations are called 'longitudinal vibrations'. It is by vibrations of this kind that the wind instruments make their sounds. The longer the tube, the slower the vibrations and the lower the note.

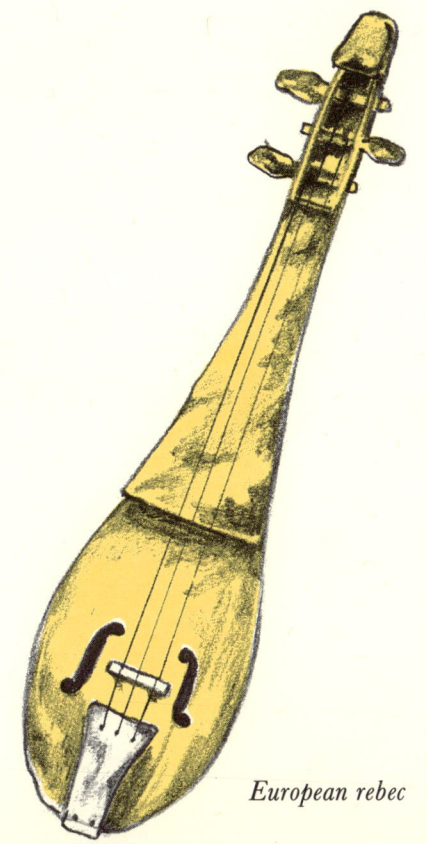

European rebec

With this in mind it is easy to understand the formation of the orchestra. It explains why the deeper harmonies of the strings come from the unwieldy double-bass, while the more lilting melodies are given to the violins. It explains the contrast between the bird-like notes of the slender piccolo and the bass of the bassoon; the shrill tunefulness of the trumpet and the resonant sound of the massive tuba. It tells why the most thunderous rhythm comes from the big drum and why the harp has so graceful a shape to provide for strings of widely varying length.

Double-bass player

DIFFERENT TYPES OF INSTRUMENT

Usually the instruments of the orchestra are divided into three classes: string, wind and percussion. Sometimes keyboard instruments are regarded as a fourth class. But to do so is deceptive in spite of being convenient. The organ, with its array of pipes blown by a bellows, is in reality a wind instrument. The keys are nothing more than a means of directing the wind from the bellows to the right pipes. Similarly, the piano is a stringed instrument. Instead of being plucked by the fingers,

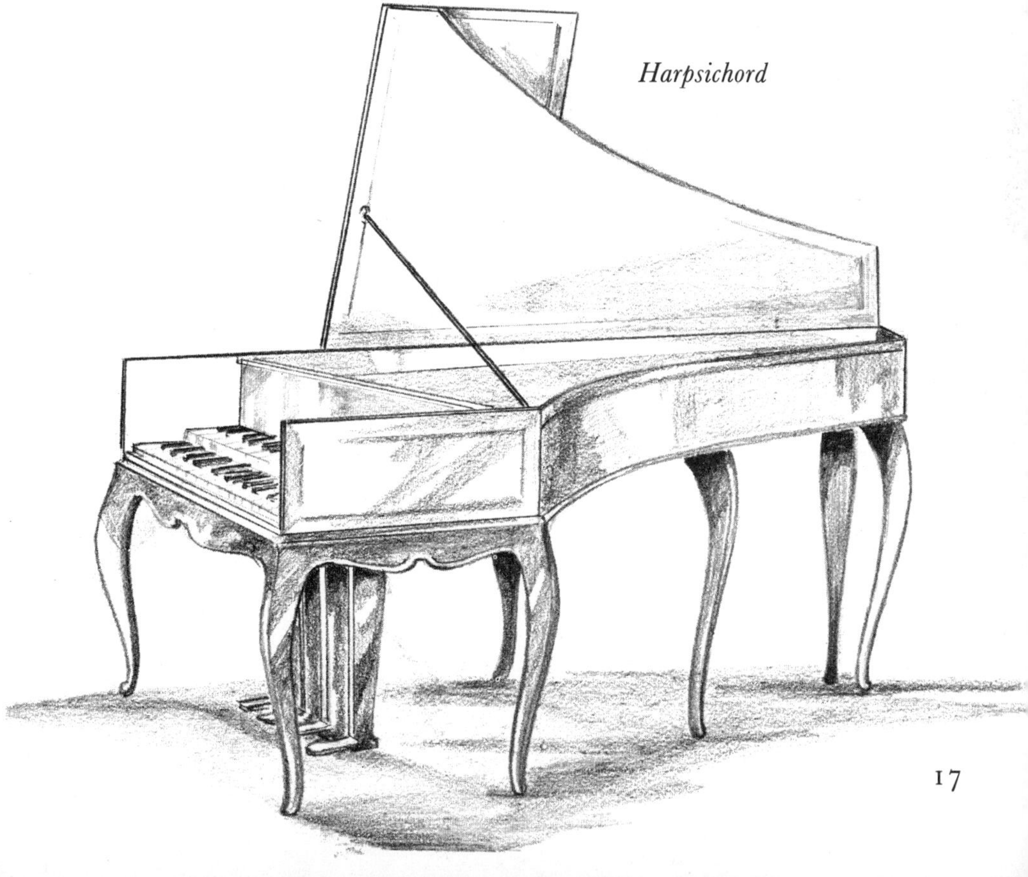

Harpsichord

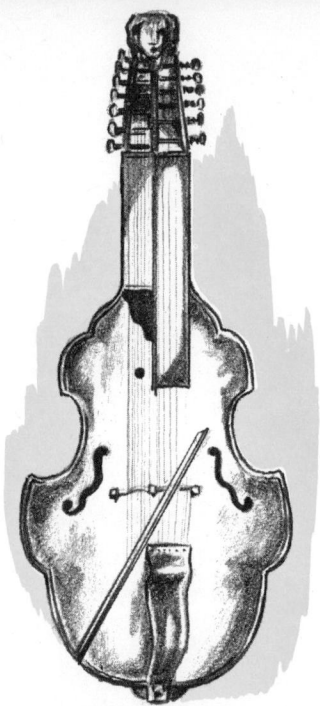

Viola di fagoto (or viola bastarda of the eighteenth century)

as with the harp, or stroked by a bow, as with the violin, the strings are struck by hammers.

During the past forty years a new complication has been introduced, the electronic organ. This, too, is a keyboard instrument. By means of electrical devices it can imitate the tones of just about any other instrument that has ever been known and some that it is to be hoped never will be! At present the electronic organ is not used in the orchestra; but its possibilities are so great that only the boldest of prophets would dare to foretell its future.

On the whole it is simpler to think of keyboard instruments as a separate class. Why all the other instruments of the orchestra are classed as either strings, wind or percussion is obvious when you watch them being played.

THE STRINGED INSTRUMENTS

Of stringed instruments there are two kinds: those that are plucked and those that are played with a bow. Let us think of the bowed instruments first. Since 1600 the bowed instruments used in a modern orchestra have scarcely changed at all. Towards the end of the sixteenth century they were brought to such perfection that nobody has been able to improve upon them. They all belong to the same family whose ancestor was the *vielle*, often known as the *fiedel*, which is known to have been played at least a thousand years ago. It was a favorite of the Welsh bards of olden times.

The vielle was probably the first European instrument to be played with a bow. The spade-shaped body it then had was later replaced with one shaped as an ellipse. Above this was a narrow neck. The five strings were carried over the body and tightened by pegs in a box at the top of the neck. The performer held the instrument in front of him and supported it on his

Vielle à archet, thirteenth-century instrument of the Troubadours

thigh or knee. A big improvement was made when the body was curved inward at the waist so that the bow could move more freely and play each string individually. Later still the body was replaced by a sounding-box pierced with holes to give it resonance.

This instrument had two children that survived. First was the *viola da braccio* (arm) which was supported on the shoulder and had four strings; the other was the *viola da gamba* (leg) which rested on the ground between the player's knees and had six strings. From these two have come the family we all know so well: the small violin and viola that are supported on the shoulder of the player; and the violoncello and double-bass that rest on the ground, because of their size.

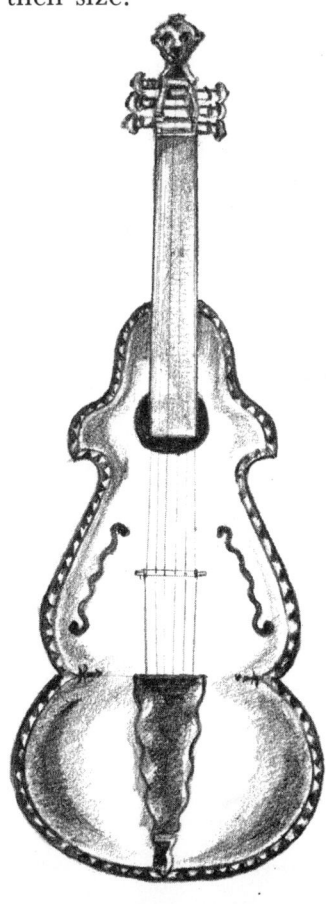

Viola da braccio (with four strings) eighteenth century, and Viola da gamba sixteenth century

Undoubtedly the smallest of them all, the violin, is queen. It is usually given the leading part when strings are playing together.

The strings of the violin are made of catgut, and the bow of horsehair. The hollow wooden shell, fourteen inches in length, is beautifully curved inward at the waist, and has flat sides while the front and back are slightly convex. The front, known as the 'table', is pierced by two *f*-shaped slits. This adds to the richness of the sound.

Four strings are led from the base of the box, over a bridge and finger-board to a peg-box. Here they are attached to pegs which, by being twisted, can tighten or loosen the strings until they have exactly the right pitch. The strange caterwaulings that come from an orchestra at the beginning of a concert are mostly caused by the violinists tuning up.

Differing from each other in thickness and in tension, the strings consequently differ in pitch. By pressing the strings against the wood with the fingers of his left hand the player can raise the pitch of each. With the instrument resting on his shoulder and tucked under his chin, he draws the bow backwards and forwards across the strings or plucks the strings with his fingers to produce a staccato sound. The violin is made of about seventy pieces of wood that are held together by glue alone. It is surprising that it holds together when the strings are tightened; but it seems strong enough. It seldom happens, if ever, that a violin drops to pieces on the platform.

Violin bow

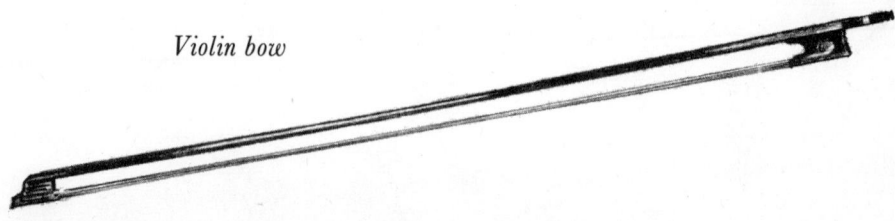

Violin, front, back and scroll

Above all instruments the violin is loved for its purity, its sweetness and its capacity for expressing every mood. Played by a master it is one of the most deeply moving of instruments. It was in North Italy and the Tyrol that it was first brought to perfection. Some of the finest violins ever made came from this region.

In Cremona there was a family of violin-makers who became famous for producing instruments of astonishing quality and mellowness. Andrea Amati was the first. His two sons, Antonio and Girolamo, inherited his wonderful craftsmanship. Girolamo's son, Nicola, taught it to a young apprentice, Antonio Stradivarius, who is still remembered as the world's greatest maker of violins. Born in 1644, he lived to the age of ninety-three and continued making violins until the year of his death. He is believed to have produced altogether 1,116 instruments, including a few violas and cellos. They have never been surpassed. Even today, the world's finest performers are proud and thrilled to hold a 'Strad' in their hands.

With a shell sixteen and a half inches in length, the viola is slightly larger than the violin and consequently has a lower pitch. For this reason it is sometimes called the 'alto' or the 'tenor' and it plays in the orchestra a role similar to that of the voices with the same names in the choir. Its deeper tones have warmth and richness. Although for playing solos it has never been as popular as the violin, it was the favorite instrument of the great composer, Brahms. Both Berlioz and Hindemith wrote solo parts for it. This, too, is held in the left hand and rested on the shoulder.

Pablo Casals, cellist

Deeper in tone by an octave is the violoncello, usually called for short the cello. About twice the size of the violin it is rested on the floor and held between the knees. Although so much larger and held differently it is constructed, tuned and played in much the same way as the violin and the viola. While the cello is hardly the best of instruments for skittishness and

gaiety, it cannot easily be bettered for the solemn, haunting melody. Rossini, Beethoven, Brahms, Schumann, Dvorák, d'Albert and many other composers have given it prominence and written solos for it. One of the most outstanding of modern instrumentalists, Pablo Casals, is a cellist.

above *Home of Stradivarius, now demolished*

Biggest of all the four, the double-bass, or contra-basso, is pitched an octave below the cello and in orchestral works is frequently used simply to double the cello part. The strings are so thick and heavy that the assistance of steel cogwheels is needed in tuning them. It is only a century since the number of strings it should have was settled. After long experiments with five and three strings it ended with four, like its sisters. As an accompaniment to other instruments it is ponderously impressive but Beethoven, Verdi and Strauss have all given it solo passages.

Egyptian woman playing harp, c. *1500* BC

Only one stringed instrument remains to be described: the harp. This is quite different from the others in origin, shape and method of playing, being plucked with the fingers like the guitar and the mandolin. To play it with a bow would be impossible.

The harp came to Europe from the Middle East, where it had figured in many legends. In early centuries the Irish had a special love for it and included it in their national coat of arms.

European frame harp

But the harp with which the young David soothed the madness of King Saul and that the minstrel boy had when he went to war 'with his wild harp slung behind him' have little resemblance to the massive piece of furniture that graces the concert platform nowadays. Only a giant could sling that over his back.

Not until a hundred and fifty years ago did the harp take its present form. A Parisian instrument-maker, Sebastian Erard, then built the first double-action pedal harp.

Like the harps of olden times this consisted basically of a sounding-box, a pillar which is often richly carved and ornamented, and a curved neck connecting the two. This gives it a triangular shape. The strings are stretched from the sounding-box to the neck and are tuned by pegs in the neck.

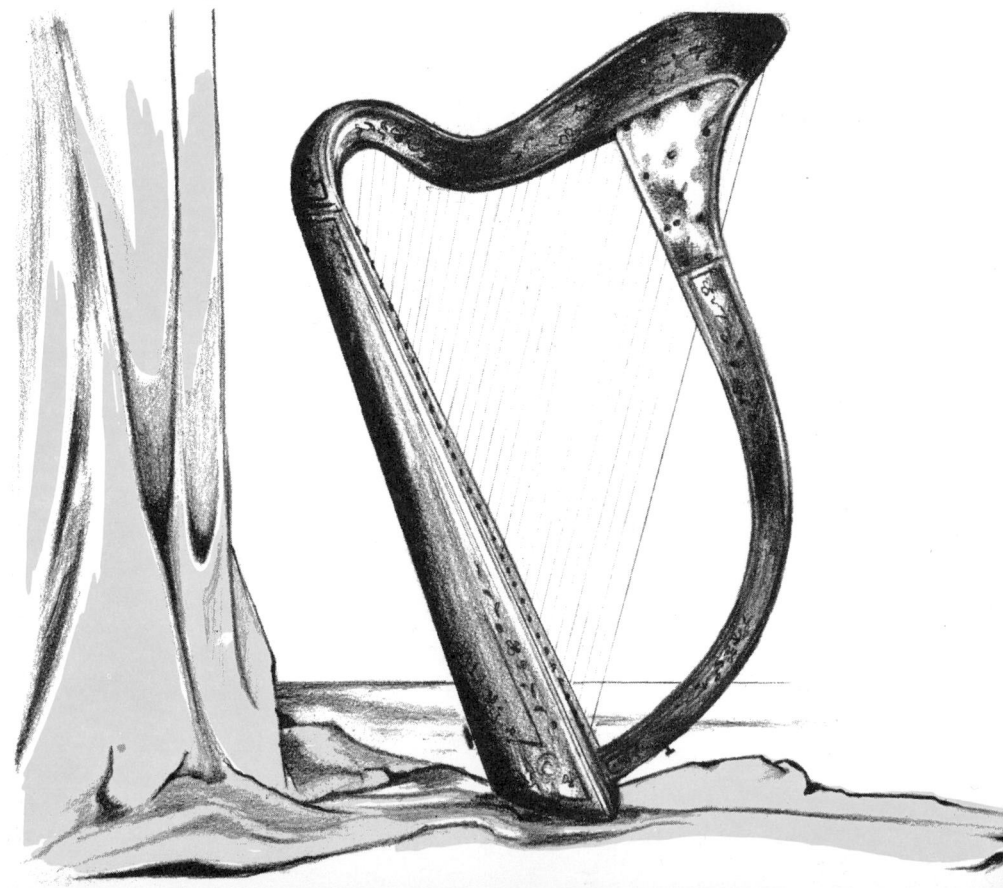

Erard's great invention was an arrangement of seven pedals with a simple mechanism for shortening the strings. When a pedal is half depressed it raises by a semitone the pitch not only of a single string but of the strings tuned to the same note through all the octaves. The harp has forty-seven strings, covering six and a half octaves. To assist the player in finding his way among them the C strings are colored red and the F strings blue.

Few people, whether music-lovers or not, can resist the cascades of sweetness that fall from this instrument. Much used for solo playing it also blends exceptionally well with the brass instruments of the symphony orchestra. Wagner gave it great prominence in the music of his operas. Unfortunately, it is one of the costliest of instruments and far beyond the pockets of most people unless they intend playing it professionally. Even then the cost and the difficulty of carrying about so large an instrument discourage would-be harpists. As a result the demand for it is small. Harps are manufactured by only a few firms in the United States and Europe.

Lute-player, fifteenth century

Twelfth-century carving, showing cornett

WIND INSTRUMENTS

Wind instruments have always been divided into two classes: wood and brass. During recent years this division has become incorrect. Flutes, for instance, are nowadays often made of metal. Clarinets are frequently made of plastic. Brass instruments are sometimes silver plated. On rare occasions a presentation model is made of solid silver. But whatever the material, the distinction between the two types is real and important. They differ unmistakably both in tone and volume and in the type of music for which they are suitable.

Another distinction is that between reed instruments and flue instruments. In the former the sound is produced by blowing air over a thin strip of cane (the reed) fixed in the mouthpiece, causing it to vibrate. In a double reed instrument

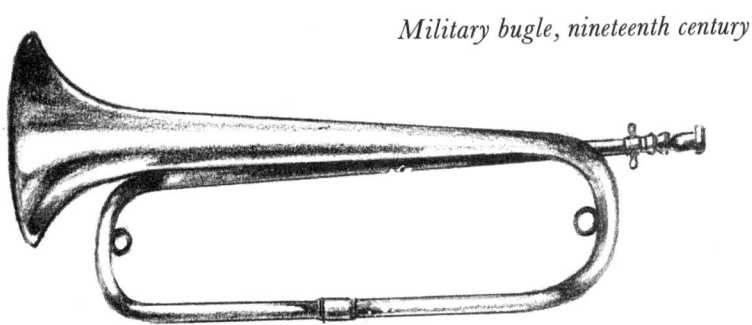

Military bugle, nineteenth century

29

two reeds are arranged with a narrow slit between them. Under the pressure of the air the two reeds vibrate together, opening and closing the slit as they do so. This allows the air to enter the tube in an interrupted stream. All brass instruments are, in effect, double reed instruments: but the movements of the lips replace the vibrations of the cane reeds. It might be said that in brass-wind instruments the human lips are the reeds. In a flue instrument there is no reed and the vibration is caused by blowing across the mouthpiece.

As in stringed instruments, the longer the string the lower the note, so in wind instruments, the longer the tube the lower the note. In the wood section the pitch can be raised by boring a hole in the side of the tube. This allows the air to escape and has the same effect as if the tube were cut off at this point. In the brass section the pitch can be lowered by adding extra lengths of tubing. As we shall see, there are various methods of doing this.

One term that is of vital importance to wind players is *embouchure*, which comes from the French word for mouth, *la bouche*. It has two meanings. First, it denotes the mouthpiece itself. Second, it denotes the way the player applies his lips to the mouthpiece. To apply them correctly takes long practice. A good set of teeth is a help. Among teachers and students of wind instruments the word *embouchure* is frequently in use.

Oboe reed

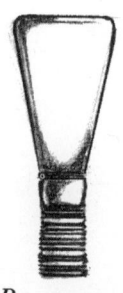
Bassoon reed

Trumpet mouthpiece

Harpist

THE WOODWIND

Now let us look at the woodwind instruments. The flute is one of the smallest and is usually made of boxwood or ebony and sometimes of metal. The sound is made by blowing across the embouchure which is placed on the side of the instrument.

The flute had a history of many centuries in the East before it came to Europe during medieval times. At first it was provided with six finger-holes to shorten the tube and raise the pitch, note by note. It was often associated with the drum and

Carving—Indian flautist, second century AD

Military fife player, eighteenth century

became popular among the military, especially the Swiss soldiers. For this reason it came to be known as the *Schweizerpfeiff* or 'Swiss Pipe'. Our own fife and drum bands are an echo of this phase of the flute's story and it is easy to see how the word 'fife' was derived.

In the seventeenth century the flute was given a key for the little finger in addition to the six finger-holes, and later still was provided with two more keys. In this form it was brought into the opera orchestra and was also the favorite instrument of a famous amateur musician, King Frederick the Great of Prussia.

Further improvements continued to be made until it became an instrument with eight keys. But this long series of developments had not been systematic. The flute was far from having reached perfection. About the middle of the last century a German performer, Theobald Boehm, decided to reconstruct it scientifically. With the aid of a physicist he re-designed the instrument in accordance with the principles of acoustics, which is the science of sound. This meant altering the size of the holes and also changing their positions.

Although this gave the notes greater clarity and purity and ensured that they were correctly pitched, it made the holes almost impossible to reach, especially since there were now so many of them. To solve this problem Boehm devised an intricate and ingenious mechanism. He covered some of the holes

Modern flute (with Boehm system)

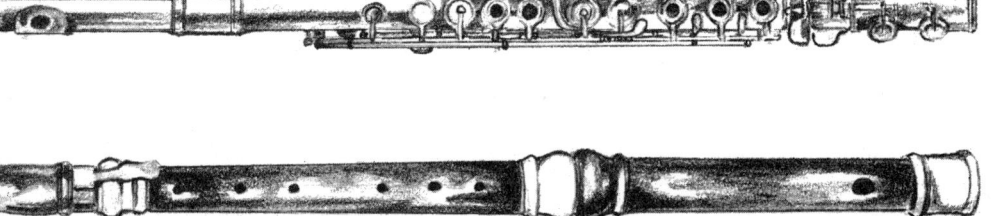

Early flute, sixteenth century

with ring-keys and connected them by thin metal rods with key-covers over the holes that were out of reach. With the aid of this mechanism the player had perfect control over his instrument.

Since these changes compelled all performers who adopted Boehm's flute to re-learn their fingering many of them were hostile to it. But its excellence ensured its success in spite of them. Boehm's flute is the one played in orchestras today. What is more, his sytem has been applied to other instruments as well.

Piccolo is the Italian word for 'little' and is used as a pet-name for small children. In the orchestra the piccolo is the baby sister of the flute. Although only about half the size it is unfortunately about double the price because of the delicacy of the workmanship that goes into it. Being smaller, it is also a clear octave higher than the flute. While built on similar principles, whereas the flute is shaped as a perfectly straight pipe, the piccolo narrows slightly towards the end. Its embouchure is the same. Both are flue instruments and have no reed. In the orchestra the piccolo is used for special effects because of its peculiarly shrill and piercing tone.

Piccolo and player

Clarinet and player

How the clarinet first came into existence is uncertain but it derives its name from the clarion sound of its higher notes, which bear some resemblance to those of the trumpet. The lower notes, by contrast, are rich and full.

It was not until the eighteenth century that the popularity of the clarinet became widespread and it was included in the orchestra. When Boehm brought his great improvement to the flute it was applied to the clarinet with similarly excellent results. The clarinet now has thirteen keys and has been so developed that it can be played comfortably in all scales. Formerly it was necessary for a player to carry at least two clarinets about with him if he were to be sure of being able to play any music set before him. Some players still believe that there is an advantage to be gained by doing this, but it is no longer essential. The clarinet is one of the larger of the wood-wind instruments and is actually made in about twenty different sizes. It has a single reed set flat inside the mouthpiece.

Of all instruments, there are few better examples than the clarinet of the infinite care and craftsmanship that go into the making of a first-class model. Even when they are turned out in scores by modern machinery their manufacture is still an object-lesson in the meaning of loving care.

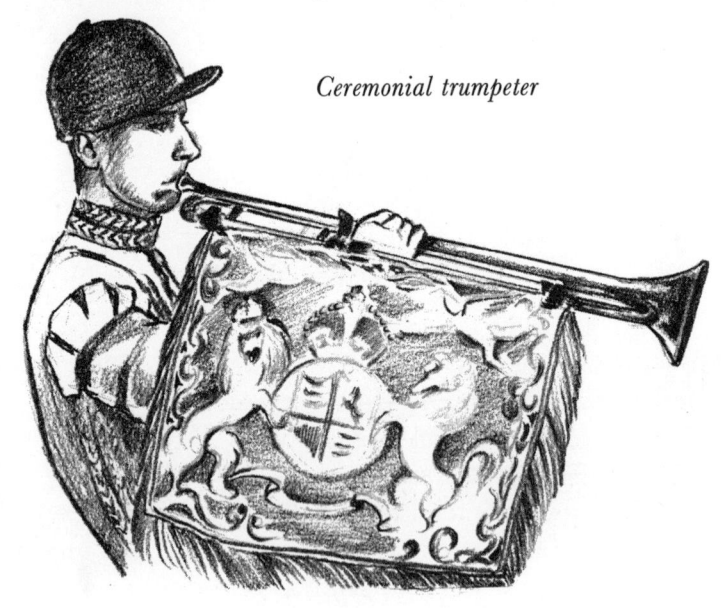

Ceremonial trumpeter

African blackwood, from which the best British clarinets are made, is found in the forests of Zambia. Growing to a height of twenty-five feet, the Mpingo tree from which the wood comes is sparsely scattered among many other kinds of timber. To find good specimens often needs a long search. Only the center of the tree is suitable for use. This has to be shipped eight hundred miles over rough tracks to the coast for shipment to England.

Recorder

In the factory ninety-seven per cent of this is thrown out as waste. The remaining three per cent has then to be stored for six months for seasoning. When, at last, it comes to actual manufacture, the clarinet comprises 295 parts which require 2,361 operations to make.

Fortunately, the plastic models now available are of excellent quality and much less expensive. Nobody but a highly experienced performer is likely to be able to use the more costly instrument to the best advantage. Another benefit of plastic is that less care is needed to keep it in good order. Plastic is not liable to the warping that threatens even the finest timber. A warning against models made of ebonite may not be out of place. They are brittle and tend to break easily.

A great conductor, Sir Henry Wood

Like the simple recorder, so popular in schools nowadays, the clarinet is a transposing instrument. This means that the musical score prepared for the player is always based on the key of C, whereas the clarinet normally used in the orchestra is in the key of B-flat. All the time he is fingering the keys the performer has to accomplish a little feat of mental acrobatics and pretend that the score is written a major second lower than it is. The note he reads will not represent the note he plays.

Similar in size to the clarinet, the oboe, too, may be made either of African blackwood or of plastic. It is a double reed instrument with the reeds protruding slightly so that they can be taken between the lips. Although difficult to play really well, it is much easier if the reed is carefully selected, well seasoned and properly cut.

Originally the oboe was a development, in the seventeenth century, of an old and much cruder instrument, the *shawm*. It was then given the French name, *hautbois* (highwood), which crossed the Channel as *hautboy* and was soon afterwards corrupted to 'oboe'. At first it had six finger-holes and three keys. So great was its popularity that Handel composed extensively for it.

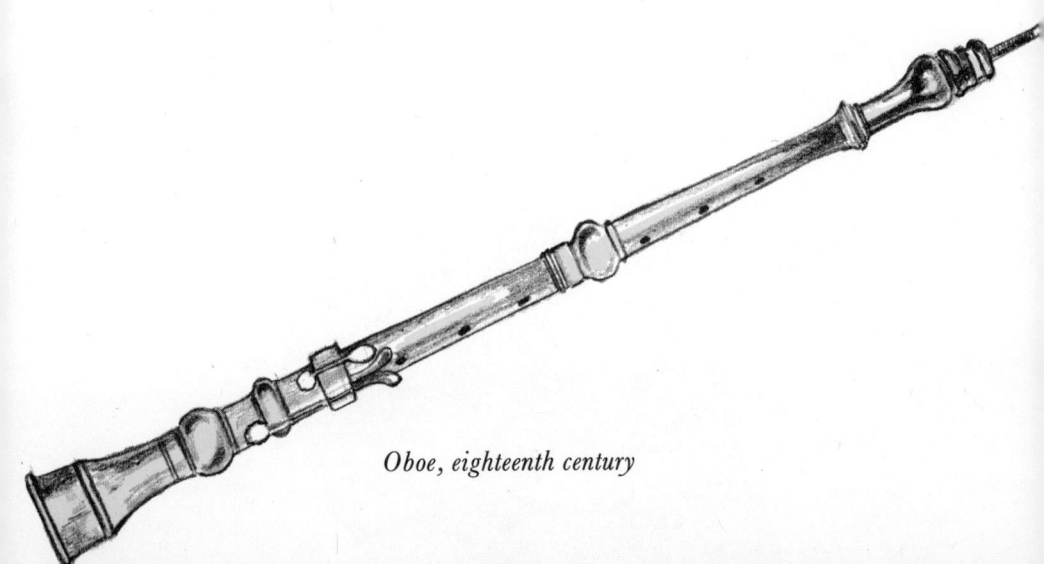

Oboe, eighteenth century

Modern oboe and player

Boehm's inventions were applied to the oboe. By this time the number of keys had risen to fourteen, but afterwards development continued faster than ever and the mechanism became more than ever complicated. This process reached its climax in 1880 when the Parisian *Conservatoire* model was constructed. Never surpassed, this is the model now in use.

Cor anglais *or English horn*

The English 'horn' is so called because it used to be curved. But the modern instrument is straight, like the oboe, and it is keyed and played in the same way, being often described as the 'alto oboe'. It is pitched lower and is a transposing instrument. A pear-shaped bell gives it a gentle, melancholy tone. Schumann and Wagner used it to express the more languid feelings and Franck used it for solo passages.

Robert Schumann and Richard Wagner

Last in the woodwind list comes the massive bassoon, no less than eight feet four inches long. This great size may be why the bassoon player is often made the object of the good-humored wit of the other members of the orchestra. The deep, impressive, mysterious quality of the tone may be another reason for this. Invariably made of maple or sycamore it is fashioned entirely by hand and a good model is a superb example of fine craftsmanship.

Since the tube is bent double the bassoon has a resemblance to a bundle of sticks and the Italians call it the *fagotto*. In the older English writers it is referred to as the *curtall*. The sound is produced by a double reed attached to a metal crook jutting from what appears to be the side of the instrument but is, in fact, one end of the doubled tube. As its present name implies it is the bass of the woodwind section.

Ludwig van Beethoven

Originating in the eighteenth century, as it gained in popularity it received technical improvements similar to those of the other woodwind instruments. By the time Beethoven wrote it had eight keys and a range of three octaves. There was at one time tremendous rivalry between German and French makers. In the end it was the German designs that won their way in this country. Bassoons have been made with as many as twenty-two keys.

One important point to be noted about all woodwind instruments is the constant care they need. During the first two years of their lives they are particularly liable to cracking if subjected to rapid variations in temperature. They should never be exposed to extremes of cold or heat and before being played should be warmed up gradually. After use they should be thoroughly pulled through and wiped dry, with special attention to the joints and the mouthpiece. The mechanical parts need a slight application of lubricating oil from time to time. If such precautions are taken these instruments will enjoy a long and honorable life and will fully retain their musical qualities.

Bassoon-player

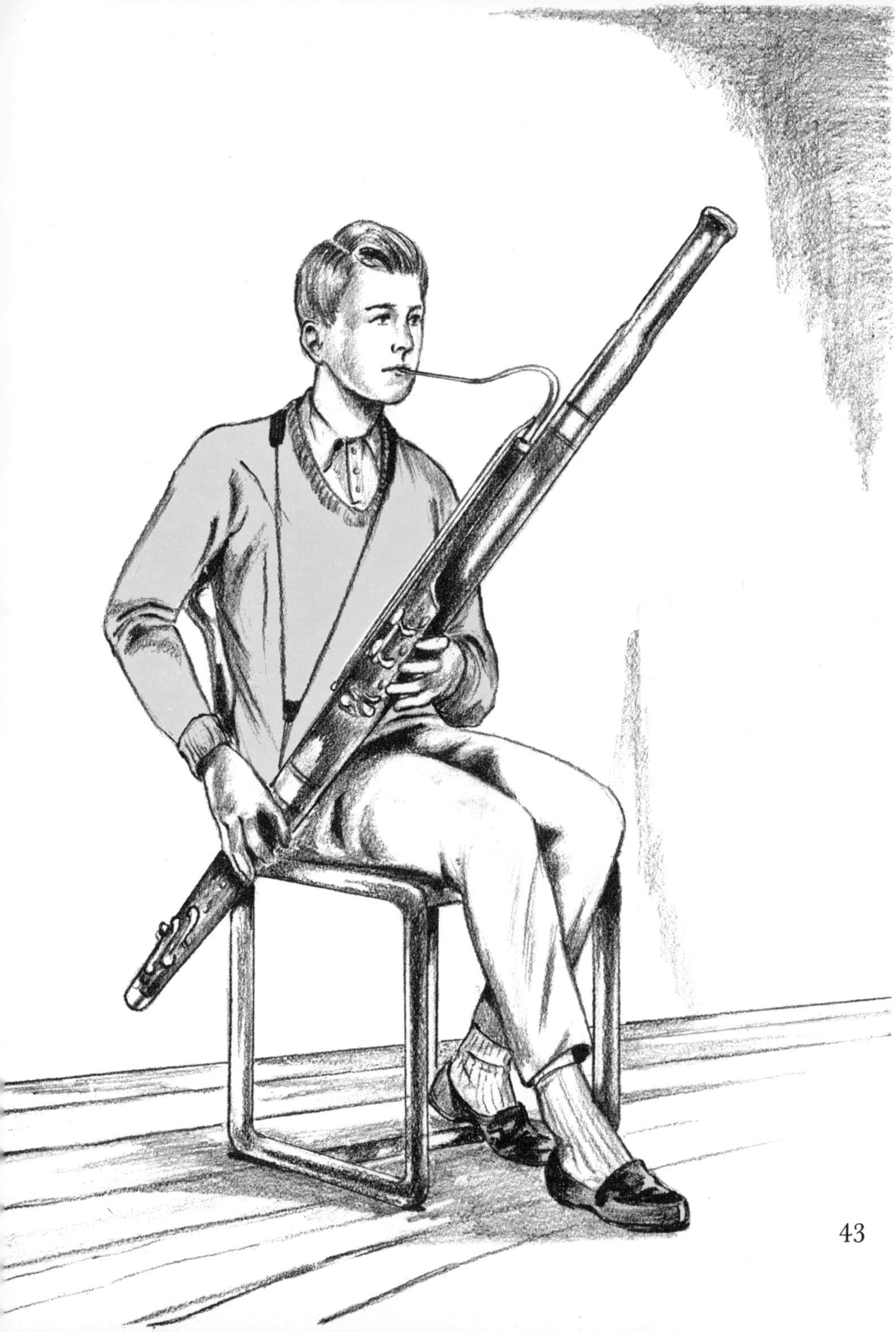

INSTRUMENTS OF BRASS

Now turn to the brass instruments, with their martial and rousing sound so closely associated with great State occasions. The air column in the tube is set in motion by the vibration of the lips through a cup-shaped mouthpiece. For any brass instrument selection of the mouthpiece is important because different players need slightly different shapes. The right pitch is obtained partly by the manipulation of the player's lips and breath but partly, also, by the length of the tube. With one exception all the brass instruments of the orchestra have three valves by means of which extra loops of tubing can be brought into operation, so increasing the range.

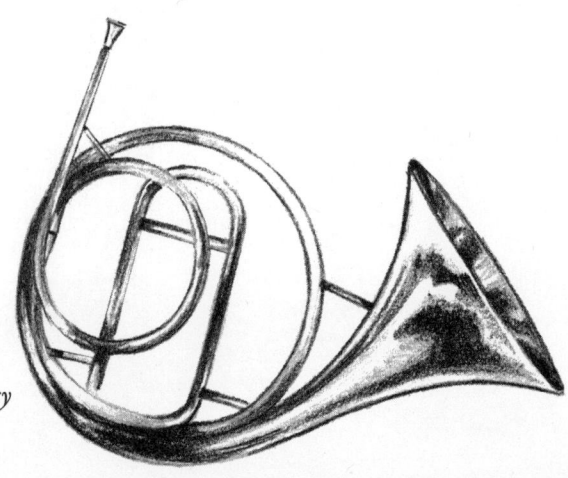

Hunting-horn

Early horn, nineteenth century

The French horn is known as one of the trickiest of wind instruments to play and is easily recognisable by the coil of its tubing. The difficulty is in hitting the right note. Performers often seem to hesitate a little when producing the first note. For a moment their uncertainty is noticeable. They are, in fact, making sure they have the correct pitch. But when played well the French horn expresses an unusually wide range of emotions, from warm tenderness to the more passionate or the harsher feelings.

This horn in the eighteenth century developed from the coiled hunting-horn, to which were added a mouthpiece and a wide bell. By introducing extra lengths of tubing as required the pitch could be altered and it was discovered also that the pitch could be lowered either a semitone or a whole tone by inserting the right hand into the bell. The addition of valves at a later date made it into the instrument we now know. Stopping the bell with the hand is still used as a means of producing special effects.

Horn-player

Eastern trumpeters—in Tibet

The trumpet is one of the most ancient instruments. It is mentioned in Chinese records as far back as 2000 B.C. It was brought to Europe in the eleventh century by the Saracens. Consisting at that time of a long, slender tube from which a banner richly embroidered with a coat of arms could be hung it tended to be the instrument of royal households and of heraldry. Later, for the sake of convenience, the tube was bent into the shape of a flattened loop as we know it now. The addition of valves brought it to perfection.

Trumpeter

Closely related to the trumpet is the trombone, the only brass instrument without valves. In Italian the word *trombone* means the 'great trumpet'. In England it used to be known as the *sackbut*, a word derived from two Spanish words meaning 'pull out the inside'. This is a descriptive name because the trombone does have a sliding section that is pulled backward and pushed forward like a telescope to shorten or lengthen the tube and raise or lower the pitch.

There are seven positions for the slide and the player needs long practice to acquire the skill that enables him to hit them correctly at the first attempt. Once the principle of the trombone was discovered the instrument was perfected so rapidly that it has hardly changed at all for over four centuries. It is distinguished by its impressive solemnity and its power.

Among the brass family the big brother is the tuba. Designed similarly to the trumpet its great size enables it to play the lowest bass notes and as a consequence it is often known as the 'bass'. Usually it has five valves but may have three, four or six. It has the appearance of a magnified trumpet.

Tuba

Trombone

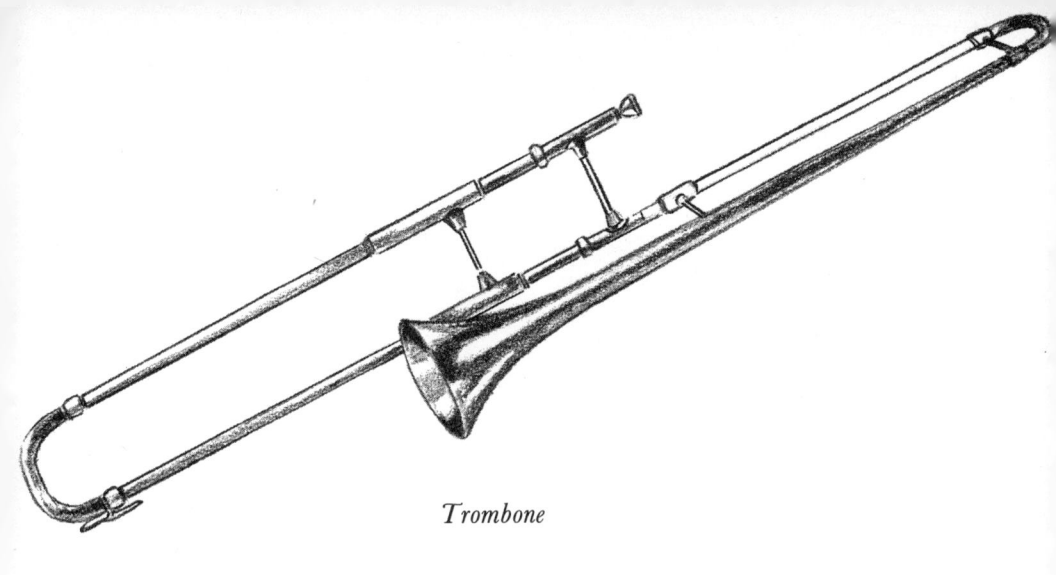

Other brass instruments are the soprano cornet, tenor horn, baritone and euphonium. These do not differ in principle from the trumpet and tuba but only in size and pitch.

Players of brass instruments need a good physique as well as a powerful pair of lungs. The strain of playing for a long time can be considerable: but it is worth putting up with this for the sake of the great satisfaction to be enjoyed by playing them well.

Moving parts on these instruments must be protected and kept free by constant lubrication. It is also important to keep them clean since dirt and mould will clog the valves as well as being unhygienic. After use the inside of the instrument should be washed with warm water and the mouthpiece cleansed with mild disinfectant. When not in use the instrument should be protected by a velvet cover. Serious dents can affect the intonation but fortunately they can be smoothed out in the repair shop.

Glockenspiel

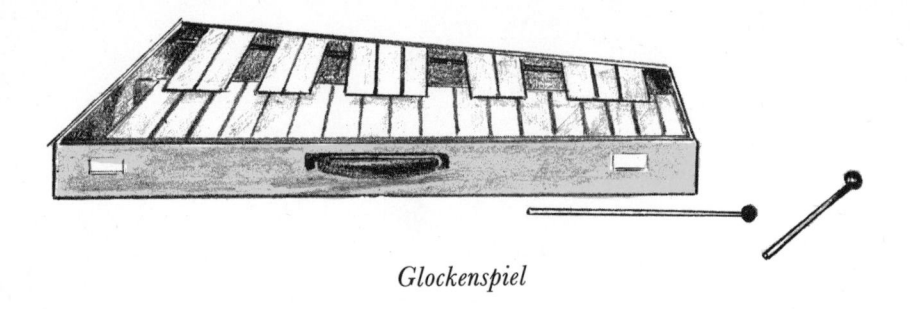

PERCUSSION

Percussion instruments also can boast an ancient and honorable lineage. The people of the Stone Age used to fashion primitive drums by stretching skins over earthenware bowls. From time immemorial the tribesmen of Africa have talked to each other at a distance by means of a code beaten out on drums.

It is the kettledrum or tympanum that is most distinctively orchestral. This, too, was favored by the Saracens who introduced it to Europe. The princes and generals of Germany then took it up enthusiastically for military purposes. Indeed, it seems to have had snob value among them because nobody less than a baron was supposed to possess one! As a creator of powerful rhythms, whether for troops on the march or for dancing, no instrument can surpass the drum.

Why this instrument should be named the kettledrum is obvious at first sight. The skin is stretched over a bowl which looks like an old-fashioned copper cauldron. The player uses drumsticks with soft heads to strike the skin. In all instruments of this kind the pitch rises as the skin is more tightly stretched: it falls if the tension is relaxed or if thicker skin is used.

With the modern kettledrum this effect is gained by a system of pedals that stretch or relax the skin when required. So efficient is this system that the instrument now has a range of an octave, and all the tones and semitones can be played quickly and correctly. While the timpani, as a set of kettledrums are generally called, are not instruments for rapid passages, slow melodies can be played on them with fine effect. Usually in an orchestra there are three kettledrums, but Berlioz scored one composition for as many as eight.

Kettledrum and bass drum

Drum sticks

Although copper is the traditional material of the shell, modern manufacturers are using modern materials as a substitute. Timpani are now available with fibre glass shells. These have the advantage not only of being less expensive but also lighter in weight and therefore easier to move about. They are not easily dented. If, in addition, plastic is used instead of skin for the head it is not as subject to damage from damp or from changes in the temperature.

By contrast with the timpani, the snare drum has straight sides and a skin stretched over both ends. Against the lower 'head' are stretched strings of catgut that rattle against the skin as the drum is beaten with wooden sticks. From this we have the inspiring roll that seldom fails to give us a thrill whenever we hear it. In producing this effect the drummer's hands move with such precision and rapidity that they can hardly be seen to be moving at all. Incessant practice gives him such control over the muscles of his forearms that the beat comes with the regularity of the ticking of a watch.

Snare drum

But the bass drum is the giant. With its shell made of wood and its two heads of vellum, it is struck by the knob of a stick padded with felt. Its deep, explosive boom is unmistakable.

Included among the percussion instruments are a number of simple devices that are brought in occasionally to provide some special effect. The cymbals, for instance, consist of two metal plates which, when struck together, yield a clashing, barbaric sound. Castanets, beloved of Spanish dancers, differ little from the toy castanets that children play. They are held between the fingers and rattled together in the same way, but are made of hardwood. The modern orchestral player has the aid of a short handle and a spring to ensure control. The tambourine consists of a hoop with a vellum head stretched across its middle. Pairs of light metal plates are arranged in the hoop in such a way that they jangle together when the vellum is struck with the hand. The triangle is simply a bent bar of steel struck with a beater across one of its angles. A gong is usually made of bronze and shaped like an overturned saucer. Most often it is struck with a padded hammer, and its sound is deep and resonant.

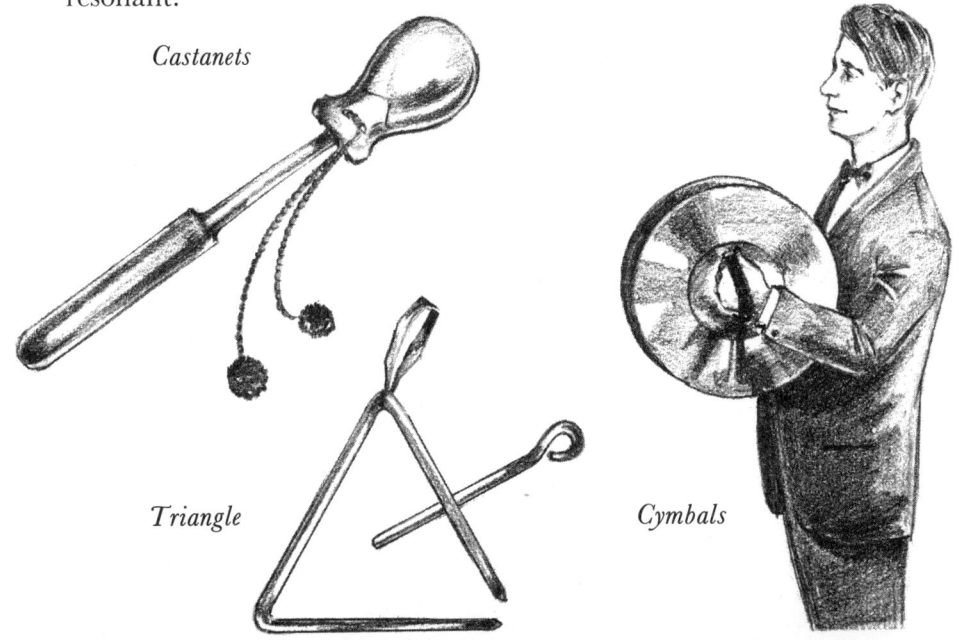

Castanets

Triangle

Cymbals

Xylophone and celesta can both be used as solo instruments. The xylophone consists of rosewood bars of graded length that are struck by the player with a beater to produce notes of different pitch. The celesta has steel bars that are struck with a hammer operated by a four-octave keyboard.

Undoubtedly, the percussion section has an imposing array of toys to play with. In some musical works the man at the centre of this collection may be expected to exercise remarkable energy and agility in turning from one instrument to another. He may, on the other hand, have to sit through a whole symphony to play only one or two bars. In that case he must watch the score with patience and concentration to make sure of coming in at the right place.

Unhappy was the tympanist who travelled all the way from London to the North of Scotland for a concert, carrying his instruments with him, to play only one note on each of the three. When the great moment came to exercise his talent he had dozed off and missed the beat! Whether the story is actually true or not, this could easily happen.

Celesta

THE PIANO

Of the various keyboard instruments the piano, which shares with the violin the honor of being the most glorious of solo instruments, is the one most important for the study of the orchestra. It had a number of forerunners, some of which are becoming popular again after having been forgotten for centuries.

One of these was the clavichord, invented towards the end of the Middle Ages, which consisted of a small, oblong box containing a set of strings. Pressure on the keys caused these strings to be struck with metal wedges. The clavichord was a beautiful little instrument for playing in a smallish room but had not enough volume for the concert hall and lacked expression.

Clavichord

Another was the spinet, whose strings were plucked by quills instead of being struck. Often known as the *virginal*, it had a delightfully sweet tone and rose to popularity during the reign of the first Queen Elizabeth. Unfortunately, it suffered from defects similar to those of the clavichord.

More important than either of these was the harpsichord which in recent years has again become fashionable as a solo instrument. This, too, was plucked by quills. But it was considerably larger than the spinet and was provided with stops and octave couplers like the organ. Later models had two keyboards, stepped one higher than the other, each of which could bring into operation a different set of strings. The harpsichord is capable of a limited range of expression, enough volume to fill a small concert hall and is distinguished by a peculiarly delicate charm. Johann Sebastian Bach and Scarlatti are among the most outstanding composers of music for the harpsichord.

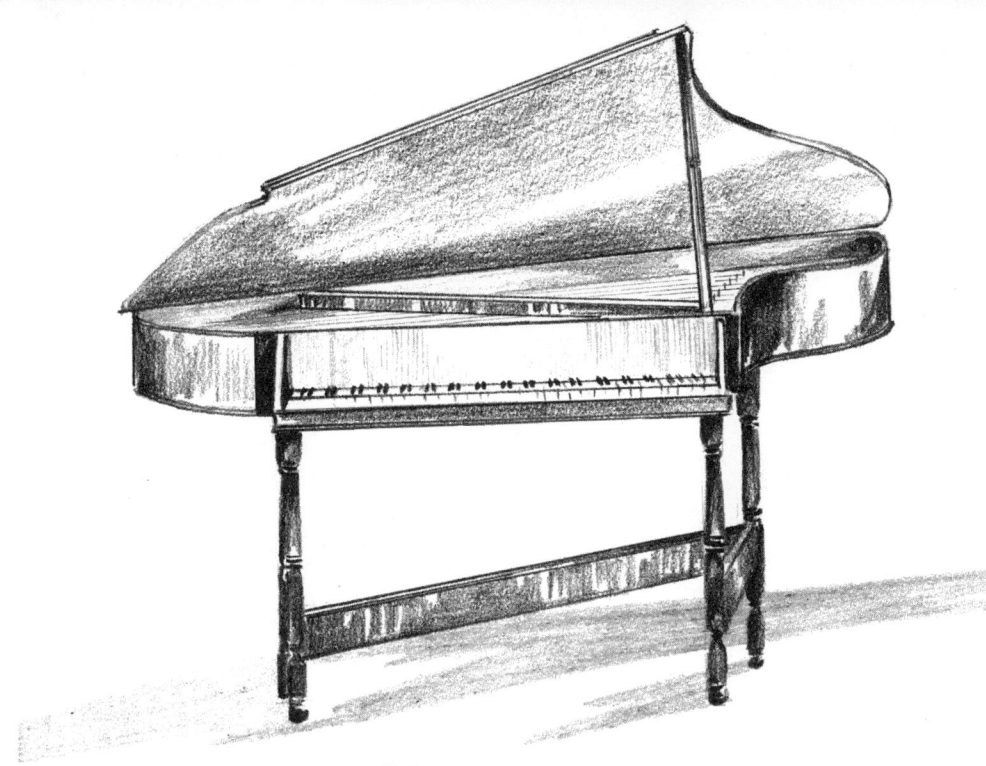

Spinet

When the piano was invented in 1709 there could be little doubt that it would win the pre-eminence. The strings are struck by felt hammers controlled from the keyboard. Part of the reason for its supremacy is the ingenious method that was devised of connecting the keys to the hammers. This enables it to be played either with lightness of touch or with strength and power to produce a wide variation of tone and volume, limited only by the skill of the performer. Two or three pedals either dampen the strings or increase the duration of their vibration.

Virginal

Pianist

In its compact and convenient form as an upright or a baby grand the piano has won its way as a family instrument for the private household. Miniature versions have been made available that are suitable even for small houses. But the massive concert grand can fill the largest concert halls. As the solo instrument in some magnificent concerto it provides both the pianist and the orchestra with a unique opportunity of displaying their virtuosity and their musicianship. Mozart and Haydn were the first of the great composers to write for it and with Beethoven, Chopin, Schumann and Liszt it became outstanding as a solo instrument. Whether the pianoforte works of these composers can ever be surpassed still remains to be seen.

Frederic Chopin

Music stand

THE GRAND ENSEMBLE

Such are the instruments, taken one by one. When they combine in an orchestra under the leadership of a great conductor they cease to be individuals and blend, instead, into one mighty and superbly sensitive instrument. As the conductor stands before a fine, professional orchestra, the players noting each movement of his hands and his baton, observing even the expression of his features, responding immediately to the slightest gesture, it is as if they were a keyboard and he the instrumentalist.

For over a century and a half the orchestra has had much the same shape as it has now. It advanced notably during the first part of the nineteenth century, that period of remarkable creativeness in the improvement of so many instruments. The orchestra assumed and kept its present shape because long experiment had shown what balance of instruments would yield the finest results.

Conductor

Nowadays an orchestra playing a symphony in a large hall may well have as many as twenty first violins with sixteen second violins playing lower in the scale to support their melody, often playing in unison with them. To ensure richness of volume and strength of rhythm it will have also five percussion instruments, eight horns, one tuba, five clarinets, five trumpets, five flutes, five bassoons, twelve cellos, five oboes, ten double basses, fourteen violas and two harps.

Today most major cities in the world have their own symphony orchestras. Annual music festivals held around the world welcome visiting orchestras and have made conductors like Arturo Toscanini, Leonard Bernstein, Serge Koussevitzky, Sir Malcolm Sargent, Sir Thomas Beecham, Eugene Ormandy, Fritz Reiner, and Bruno Walter well known in many countries and to many people.

Not all combinations are as mighty as this! Chamber music, for instance, is written for an ensemble with only one player for each part. Originally it was intended to be played in the mansions of the aristocracy and is at its most effective in a small hall. Similarly, a string quartet is exactly what its name suggests.

Full orchestra

Military bands omit the strings altogether. Can you imagine soldiers playing violins or cellos as they march to battle? Instead they concentrate on the percussion, the brass and the woodwind so as to produce a strong, marching beat and an inspiring martial sound. Brass bands too are exactly what their name implies. They are particularly suitable for amateurs and are good for open-air occasions since the sound of the brass instruments carries so well.

But the full orchestra is the monarch of all instrumental combinations. There is seldom such a sense of occasion as when it is about to play a great symphony. All the circumstances must be made to serve the one grand purpose. The hall itself almost becomes a part of the orchestra. The science of acoustics has not yet been able to guarantee the design of a hall to be perfect for the reproduction of music. If there should be a bad echo the balance of the orchestra may be disturbed and the clarity of the sound may be blurred. If the walls and ceilings are so proofed that there is no echo at all, then the instruments will seem dead and lifeless. The music may even trail away into a labyrinth of galleries and corridors.

Conductors with the touch of genius know how to allow for these possibilities and even turn them to advantage. It is the first violinist who disciplines the orchestra: the conductor controls its performance. The first violinist is the chief of staff: the conductor is the general of the army. He does far more than just beat time. He cannot be expected to play every instrument,

Military band leader

but he must understand them all. He must know their full potentialities and how to bring the best out of them. He must also understand people, because he has to inspire his team and win its loyalty. Standing, in a sense, between the orchestra and the audience, he has to link them together and create a good relationship between them.

Beyond that, he has to understand and interpret the mind of the composer. Merely to follow the score of the full orchestra is a considerable intellectual feat. To see through the marks on the paper to the intentions behind them requires a splendid gift of sympathy. All this is part of a conductor's personal equipment. An experienced, professional orchestra may be able to perform adequately in spite of a poor conductor: a truly great conductor will lead it to surpass itself.

So, with a hum of conversation and an expectant stirring, the audience waits. The instruments have tuned up and now the leader of the orchestra walks on to the platform amid mild applause to take his place at the head of the violins. There is an almost tangible silence as the conductor acknowledges with a bow the welcome of the audience and turns to the orchestra. He raises his baton. For a brief moment he looks around as if assuring himself of full mastery of the situation. He makes a swift gesture and a great event has begun.

Conductor

INDEX

Amati, Andrea, 24
Aulos, 11
Bach, Johann Sebastian, 56
Bass drum, 16, 53
Bassoon, 16, 30, 41-43
Beecham, Sir Thomas, 60
Beethoven, Ludwig van, 25, 26, 42, 58
Berlioz, Louis Hector, 24, 50
Boehm, Theobald, 33-35, 40
Brahms, Johannes, 24, 25
Buccina, 12
Bugle, 29
Casals, Pablo, 24, 25
Castanets, 53
Celesta, 54
Chopin, Frédéric, 58
Clarinet, 29, 35-38, 60
Clavichord, 55
Conductor of orchestra, 59-63
Cornu, 12
Cymbals, 53
d'Albert, Eugene Francis, 25
Doublebass cello, 16, 21, 26, 60
Dvořák, Antonín, 25
Electric organ, 18
Embouchure, 30, 32, 34
English horn, 40
Erard, Sebastian, 27-28
First violinist, 62

Flute, 29, 32-34, 60
Franck, César, 40
French horn, 45, 60
Glockenspiel, 50
Gong, 53
Handel, George Frideric, 38
Harp, 16, 18, 26-28, 31, 60
Harpsichord, 17, 56
Haydn, Joseph, 58
Hindemith, Paul, 24
Hunting horn, 44-45
Kettledrum, 50-52
Keyboard instruments, 17, 18, 55-58
Kithara, 11
Koussevitzky, Serge, 60
Liszt, Franz, 58
Lute, 28
Lyre, 10, 12, 14
Mandolin, 26
Mozart, Wolfgang Amadeus, 58
Oboe, 30, 38, 39, 40, 60
Orchestra, 12, 13, 16, 17, 18, 22, 24, 34, 44, 59-63
Ormandy, Eugene, 60
Percussion instruments, 17, 18, 50-54, 60
Piano, 17, 55, 57-58
Piccolo, 16, 34, 55
Pipe organ, 17, 56
Recorder, 13, 38
Reiner, Fritz, 60

Rossini, Gioacchino Antonio, 25
Sargent, Sir Malcolm, 60
Scarlatti, Allessandro, 56
Schumann, Robert, 25, 40, 41, 58
Snare drum, 52
Spinet, 56, 57
Stradivarius, Antonio, 24, 25
Strauss, Johann, Jr., 26
Stringed instruments, 15, 16, 17, 18, 20-28, 30
Tambourine, 53
Toscanini, Arturo, 60
Transposing instrument, 38-40
Triangle, 53
Trombone, 47-48
Trumpet, 16, 30, 35, 36, 46, 60
Tuba, 12, 16, 48, 60
Tympanum, 50-52, 54
Verdi, Giuseppe, 26
Vielle, 20
Viola, 21, 24, 25, 60
Violin, 16, 18, 21-23, 60
Violoncello, 21, 25, 60
Wagner, Richard, 28, 40, 41
Walter, Bruno, 60
Wind instruments, 17, 29-49
Wood, Sir Henry, 37
Xylophone, 54

WATERLOO LOCAL SCHOOL
MIDDLE SCHOOL LIBRARY

DATE DUE			
DEC 18			
MAR 30			
OCT 24			

781

AUTHOR: OWEN, ROBERT, Editor
TITLE: LET'S LOOK at musical instr. & the orchestra.

DATE DUE	BORROWER'S NAME	ROOM

781

OWEN, ROBERT, Editor

LET'S LOOK at musical instr. and the orchestra